The Heart of Max

by

Ina Louise Jones

Chara Press

The Heart of Max
Copyright © 2017 by Ina Louise Jones

Published in the United States of America by
Chara Press
PO Box 79
Keasbey, New Jersey 08832

Book Design by Jamie B. Banta, JamieBeeDesigns.com
Photographs © Ina Louise Jones
Photographs & Illustrations © Jamie B. Banta

Cover Design by Jamie B. Banta, JamieBeeDesigns.com
Cover Photography & Illustrations:
Jamie B. Banta (hibiscus)
Jamie B. Banta (pawprints)
Depositphotos/aletia (couple)
Depositphotos/CaptureLight (terrier)

Print ISBN: 978-1-944705-00-8
E-book ISBN: 978-1-944705-01-5
Printed in the United States of America

First Edition, 2017

Dedication

To my family and to pet lovers everywhere.

The heart has eyes which the
brain knows nothing of.

Charles H. Parkhurst

One

My Story
by Max Jones
as expressed to Ina Louise Jones

Poppi had things I couldn't play with: tubes winding around on the floor, dangling wires, a nebulizer which made a funny noise like a hair dryer at the doggie spa, and a growling air compressor that my master said sounded like a ship's turbine engine.

Of course, I adapted brilliantly to it all and even to the "No!" stuff, for I'm an Australian terrier, a small, tenacious, confident breed of canine—a unique and handsome dog, if I may say so myself.

I'm Max, and I really appreciate your taking the time to read my story. You've probably enjoyed books or movies about talking dogs before, but if any dog says he can talk, they're not telling the truth.

Yet, we doggies can relate our lives … if only people would open their hearts and imaginations …

This is my tale as understood by my owner, my friend and companion, and I think she knows me pretty well. Poppi called her Ina, but I call her "Yip" because when I yip, she always comes to me. She's really clever.

As I mentioned, I'm an Australian terrier. We're an interesting and dignified canine, originating from a mix of various terrier breeds, some say from the Yorkshire and Cairn terriers "down under"in Australia, with Silkies thrown in for good measure. I was born January 8, 2006, at a breeding and boarding facility for beautiful dogs like me on the west coast of Florida. I've been told that I am a truly special mix of terrier.

Long before my littermates and I were whelped, Poppi and Yip decided it might be a good time to get a puppy. Their home was empty of the furry and fuzzy after losing their last pet, a feline (cat), to old age. After about a year without hairy dust balls billowing across the tile, or fuzz decorating the living room furniture, they figured it was time for another pet.

They reasoned, rightly, that having the perfect dog would allow them to take those calm walks in the balmy Florida evenings, or relax while watching television with their sweet doggie at their feet, who would look lovingly and longingly into their eyes and enjoy being patted on the head or scratched under the chin after being rubbed on its tummy, but … I knew what they really needed.

On March third, almost eight weeks to the date of our birth, Poppi and Yip traveled across Florida to make their choice of available puppies.

We little ones were tiny and adorable — all real charmers and anxious for special people to take us home with them. We each wore a different colored yarn around our necks for humans to tell us apart when they came to choose a puppy. My yarn was red, and of course, I was called Mr. Red.

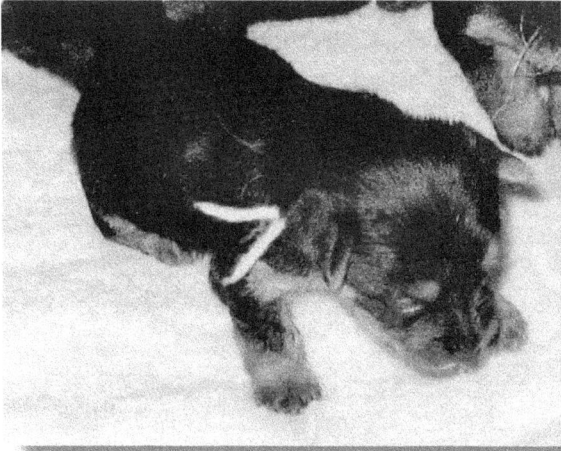

Enter John and Ina, otherwise properly known as my Poppi and Yip.

Since they were the first people to place a deposit on a puppy, they had the first choice — or so they thought. You see, I just knew I was going home with them. After all, I'm an Australian terrier, courageous, and extremely instinctive.

Yip couldn't decide between Mr. Purple, Mr. Orange, or me. She adored us all as she picked us up one at a time and kissed us on our heads and held us close to her heart.

Mr. Orange was the smallest and babyish and wanted to cuddle. Mr. Purple was the comedian, he liked to grab and pull my tail when I wasn't looking. However, the breeder agreed with Poppi that I, Mr. Red, had "the look." She also proudly announced I was the Alpha pup, always wanting to be first in checking out everything and everyone; squeaking or yipping orders from the very start. All I felt within and showed outwardly, was extreme bravery, alertness, and of course, absolute charm.

I knew my doggy mom liked me the best, 'cause she fed me first, undoubtedly because I was the most handsome. The breeder said I'd probably grow up to look more like my doggy father who had the rougher coat. My mother had the smooth, silky coat.

After being kissed on the head again and taken back to my mom and litter mates, I padded to the gate to let everyone know I wanted to be the first puppy chosen. I yipped, "Come back! Come back!"

After about forever, I heard footsteps.

"Yep! Yep! Pick me! Pick me!" Placing my front paws straight out and almost bowing down, I excitedly barked all the more.

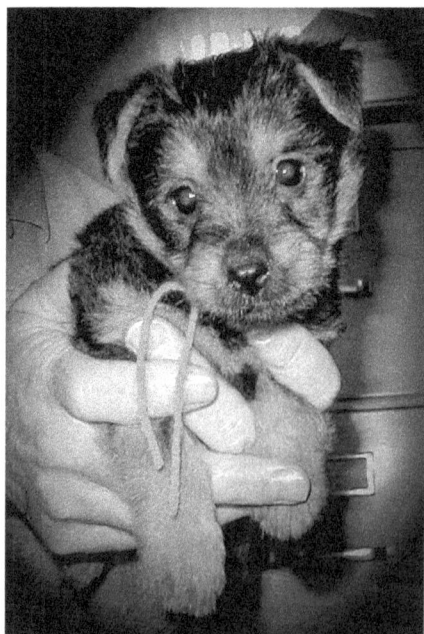

I was brought out to the large room again and found myself being lifted from the floor by big, strong hands. I looked into a man's smiling face and his happy, clear blue eyes. My Poppi.

His raspy voice breathed out, "I want this one. Call him Max."

Yip really didn't have much of a say after that, for once down on the floor, I sauntered right back to Poppi with my little tail straight up and the tips of my puppy ears flopping in sync with my jaunty and plucky stride, thinking, "Maaax. Yeaaah! I like that name."

After signing a bunch of papers and hearing about food, feeding, etc., my new people were ready to leave for parts unknown to me. Poppi gathered my "adoption" papers and Yip lifted me up to her neck and held me close. She whispered, "Let's go home, Max."

I knew these special people were the ones for me!

I opened my mouth to bark how happy I was, but all I could do was pant and let my little pink tongue hang out. My eyes were wide and bright as I headed down the path to a brand-new world and watched my birthplace get smaller and smaller. Being carried so high sure felt invigorating and exciting, and I loved seeing way beyond the fences and hedges, bouncing along, and having soft and lovely noises whispered to me.

Yip tucked me in a travel cage with a soft blue blanket and all the outside smells disappeared. I also got a small stuffed toy that smelled like my doggy mom. I guess so I wouldn't be too lonely. Being somewhat exhausted and gently joggled inside the cage, I slept all the way to my new home, except for a little sip of water about halfway.

I was off to being a great dog in every way because even as a puppy, I didn't whine or bark excessively, and I ate really well.

However, I did try my baby teeth out on Yip's hands

and arms. Of course, I was only playin' as little dogs do, but she yelped and even growled at me! I remember hearing, "No bite…no bite…" Gosh, I was just bein' a puppy, exercising my gums.

I tried exercising my gums with Poppi too, but Poppi would voice gruffly, "No!" Yip watched me like a hawk and wouldn't let me be sneaky about it either.

I figured out all those no's eventually because I'm a very good listener. I tilt my head and flip my ears as I listen to every sound Yip speaks — always.

However, by then, my pointy baby teeth that left little marks on her arms were one by one falling out! Whoa! Losing my teeth? What next? My tail? I chased it around and around to make sure it was still there. To my relief, nice big teeth replaced my lost ones. Now I could really chomp those carrots.

Before they brought me home, they put strong fences at each entrance to the kitchen; but being tiny, I did squeeze through a few times, but Poppi fixed that, too. Finally, I grew too big to slip through the slats; in fact, the gates could have held back a German shepherd. Yip used to mutter, "… thank goodness for gates."

Poppi and I did all kinds of fun stuff together. We

took walks in the backyard, rode on his golf cart, played near the pool, and dozed on the patio. Yip took care of me, but Poppi was my real master.

He scratched my back and talked funny to me. I always pointed my ears up and stared at him intently, panting a great deal to show him I approved of everything he said. All he had to do was look into my eyes, point his finger and say some noises, and I knew exactly what he wanted me to do — well, almost. We were a good team.

One thing for sure, I knew I was loved.

I got to eat the best dry food and canned food. I also got raw carrots, broccoli florets, chopped hard-boiled egg, yogurt and chopped apples, or pieces of orange slices cut up real small. Still do sometimes. When I was real little, I got raw beef soup bones from time to time — that marrow from inside was soooo good. Some days I got other stuff from the BARF diet. No, not the throw-it-up kind. B.A.R.F. means Bones And Rough Food. No bones anymore, though. I miss them.

When I was little, I jumped up a lot (still like to), and Yip tried to get me acquainted with the word "off." I also heard a bunch of other words:

"No, don't do that."
"Off…down…didn't you hear me?"
"Max, I'm talking to you."
"Off…do you have to go potty?"

"Now Max, you listen to me."
"Want a cookie?"

Gosh, she was funny, but I just blinked my eyes and panted to let her know she's important.

I loved chasing her feet, especially when she had those funny socks on—the ones with the white fluffy balls in the back? I chomped one off and ran around with it hanging out of my mouth and dove under the bed. She wasn't too pleased, but Poppi laughed so hard he had tears in his eyes. Making him laugh was one of my most important jobs, so I guess I did good. As I craftily poked my head out from under the bed to see if anyone was chasing me, Yip stole back her fluffy ball and ended the fun, but Poppi was still laughing.

My doggy parents had big long names on their pedigree papers, but I didn't have a long name. Still don't, although Yip said she could always write down, *Max*

Tasmania Terror of the House of Idiots. She always laughed about that and gave me a big hug. I knew she was only kidding, so I just panted real happy-like. Anyhow, how can you pick another name when you already have a perfect one? Max. That's me.

Being a just a young pup, I needed my immunizations, but since too much all at once was bad for my immune system and could mess me up later, that meant extra trips to the vet for the needle thingy. It must be because Australian terriers are so special. Yip and the vet meant well, but between you and me, I could pass on the needle thingy.

When I was almost six months old, Yip announced it was time I was neutered. She said that she absolutely (stressing the absolutely) didn't want any of those male terrier hormones wriggling around in my busy body! Ewww, sounded like I wouldn't want them either, but what did I know?

Back to the vet we went. Nice people there, but that needle thingy was getting old fast. I wasn't happy about feeling ouchy after an unexpected nap either, but a few days later I felt peppy enough to drag Yip out for our regular walks.

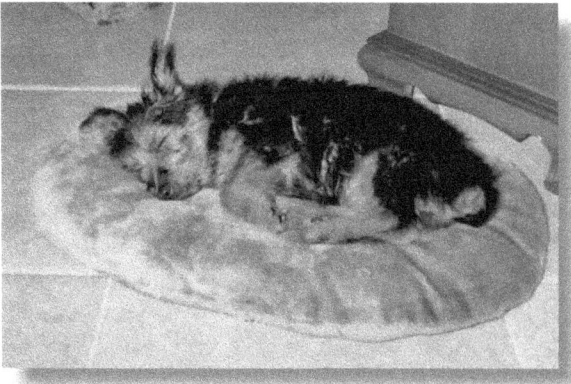

When I first got to my new home, I had what some people might call a simple mishap, but to me, it was a scary moment in my short little lifetime.

We were coming into our screened, outdoor room from visiting the soft green grass in the backyard, and as Yip turned to shut the screen door, my little legs kept walking, and I fell right into a deep, wet, blue abyss! I found out later it's called a pool.

Luckily, before I could even think, "What the…!" Yip had scooped me from the watery deep with one hand. I was dripping with the wet stuff from every hair on my body. She wrapped me in a big towel and carried me into the house. Then she plunked me into more of the wet stuff, warm this time. She called it a bath and gave me a rubdown afterward. I was exhausted. What an experience!

Not too long after that mess, I had another great crisis or 'mishap.' Since I'm a terror, ah, terrier, nothing escapes my being ever-careful and astute—except for ants, those Florida red ants.

I was walking Poppi out along the grass on our street and my attention was drawn, and very quickly I might add, to one of those white plastic coffee tops. It smelled truly fascinating, so naturally, I had to smell it real close. Only…WHAM! Before you could say "Big mistake!" those red devils had covered my face, crawled up my legs, and were making my life miserable! Poppy immediately grabbed me up into the air and rushed us back home to Yip.

Splash! Swish! Back into the pool I went, soaked and sputtering once again, trying to keep my nose up in the air to breathe as Poppi and Yip brushed off the nasty, bad ants. I hate to think what it might have been like if we'd been further from home! Towels were used, and I had to have another bath. I had only a few bites and no repercussions from the incident, but anytime I hear "Ants!" I don't touch. Lesson well learned, and boy, was I tired all the rest of the day after that episode.

When Poppi took me around the yard, he had to pull that oxygen tube-container with him all the time and it always tired him out. I don't think it was because I ran this way and that, zipping in and around the bushes, grabbing those dead hibiscus flowers or chunks of mulch, or my chasing the ducks that flew high overhead or my searching diligently for those tasty beans the rabbits always left hiding deep in the green grass.

I saw those big rabbits more than once, and I always protected Poppy and Yip from them, but when I saw armadillos for the first time, boy, was I ready for action! They were huge. I definitely had to guard my people from them. Then, there were the bad raccoons. Yip warned me about those.

On one particular morning, we were out before the sun was awake. I was taking care of business and sniffing out the neighborhood news when we spied those gray marauders, the raccoons. I was ready to take them on to protect the whole neighborhood from their invasion. Well, I tried! Once again, Yip grabbed me faster than you can say "Foiled again!" and lifted me high into the air as I wiggled and wriggled, barking and yipping as I tried to tell her, "Lemme at em!" Yip hustled us into the house real fast, she was huffing and puffing and me still wriggling.

She could hardly breathe for laughing as she set me

down in the kitchen and told Poppi the whole story. He laughed too, but I knew he was very proud of me.

My exceptional barking must have scared those raccoons away because we never found them in our yard again. I saw a black snake once, but it slithered in amongst the hibiscus bushes and trying to find it nearly drove me nuts, and I guess I drove Yip nuts because she said "No!" several times. Shucks, I could have taken on that guy too, if she'd let me.

When I was little, Yip and Poppi had quite a time trying to figure out when I needed to go to the "bathroom," as they called it. "Potty" was another word they used interchangeably. You see, I didn't understand their language too well then, and they didn't know mine so well either, so I'd really try my best to let them know when I had to go potty by dancing and staring at them.

When I first arrived, Yip would put me in the big bathtub on top of a puppy nappy to "potty" me during the night, then on a leash during the daytime. I didn't have a problem then, and she praised me for being such a good boy; but since my surgery (to rid my cute body of those hormone wriggly things), I decided that being in the tub was a no-no.

I wanted to go out where big dogs go—you know, out to the wonderful green grass, to the bushes and trees. It's an important dog job to leave messages, and I wanted to leave mine, too.

I got her up as usual after that, before the sun rolled around, and she muttered something in a foreign language as she got ready. She must have expected to take me to see the moon and stars because she had her robe and my leash right there every night, draped and dangling off my cage.

So nice out there! The moon shines on the wet grass, and the breeze blows around the aroma of flowers, orange blossoms, and other scents dogs like.

As I sat there, lifting my nose into the air, licking my upper lip and my little brain taking in the wonder of it all, I heard above the gentle rustle of the swaying palm fronds ...

"MAX! POTTY!"

Wow! That sure disturbed one's appreciation for the beauty of the moment.

Yip learned after about a month or so that I really don't go "by the book." Actually, she verbalized it quite often, but going potty was all very simple as a pup. When in the kitchen, I shook my little head, danced around, chose my favorite tile near the baby gate (I tried to oblige as best I could to get as close as possible to the outside door) and then ...

Well, after a few weeks I had Poppi and Yip pretty well-trained to take me out when I put on my "anxious" look. Things worked well for all, afterwards.

Poppi and I spent many hours on the patio by the pool. We'd go swimming in the warm weather and enjoy the fresh air. My favorite part was just laying on the top step of the pool with my tummy in the water, especially after my long walks with Yip. What a great life!

Choosing Poppi and Yip for my forever family had worked out perfectly.

Early on, I learned to jump up towards Poppi without scratching his legs, looking very needy and happy, which, naturally, I was. He'd manage to pick me up and have me sit by him, and of course, that's what I wanted. We had a rare relationship. Doggies really do love people, but people don't call it that. They call it devotion, loyalty, or being protective.

And speaking of dogs, when I was about a year old, someone suggested to my Poppi and Yip that maybe they'd want to get another puppy to keep me company. Funny thing, Poppi and Yip almost choked on their drinks!

I had a large kitchen crate that I could go into when I needed to rest, or when they had to go to a doctor, or for those "time-outs." I'd be busy playing, and Yip would announce sharply, "Okay! Max? Time-out!" And for some unknown reason, she'd plop me into the crate.

I also have a nighttime crate in the big bedroom. She used to put me to bed earlier sometimes even though I wasn't tired. I just didn't understand her thinking.

I loved being busy. One night I really wanted to have fun, and I didn't want to go to bed, so I quick snagged a magazine securely by my front teeth and ran through the house. I sprinted to the front bedroom, swiftly executing a dive into a dark hole under a tucked-up bed skirt the way only a proper Australian terrier could do, zipped deeply to the center and tore that magazine paper to confetti shreds.

That game was fun for a while and gave Yip some exercise, so a double win for me, but she eventually snagged my collar, and dragged me out with a whole big bunch of words in that foreign language again and took me promptly to bed. She kissed the top of my head (which she always does), shut my crate door, and went back into the living room to Poppi.

"Yup, he has *the look* all right," she announced. "I think you picked your soul-mate." I heard their laughter and the clink of glasses as my eyes slowly closed, and me smiling happily, looking forward to another day of a wonderful life with the Joneses.

Two

Well, it was bound to happen. One day, Yip and Poppi came to the conclusion that I needed a playmate…actually, *Yip* needed me to have a playmate. (I don't think it was in desperation, though. The more,

the merrier, right?) Her only prerequisite — *not* another terrier. Yip hit the Internet, searching the pounds, rescue organizations, and even a few breeders for another puppy.

The list was down to three rescues: a beautiful, wide-eyed (we really do love that look) female terrier, named Shannon, a male mixed-breed called Matty, and a male Poodle-mix named, of all things, Johnny. All of them were about my size, and of course, incredibly cute.

Yip and Poppi checked out Matty first, but decided against him because, as Yip said, "It just didn't feel right." I heard her cry a little because she had to leave him there.

And since she'd sworn up and down no more terriers, the lovely Shannon was really out of the question.

So they brought home the forlorn-looking Poodle-mix, Johnny-dog.

Johnny-dog was more than forlorn; he weighed less than eleven pounds, had just been neutered the night before, and he had a real nasty urinary tract infection. He'd had a real bad life before Yip found him. Poor thing! He smelled funny, too — interesting, but weird.

I really liked being an only dog, but it suddenly hit me, hey, this could be fun!

Johnny-dog tried half-heartedly to wag his tail when we met, but he wouldn't walk on his own. Gosh, those sad eyes! I licked his face to tell him the best I could that everything would be okay and he should just trust he was in good hands with Yip and Poppi.

After a vet visit within the hour of arriving home, being examined, getting antibiotics and pain pills, Yip and Poppi took the new guy and me outside to do our doggie thing in the green grass. Poor pup, Johnny-dog could hardly walk, let alone pee, so Yip just let him go wherever he stood, while I made sure to leave a message on the hibiscus bush.

Once back in the patio, Yip turned to close the screen door, but that's when disaster almost struck. I hadn't had a chance to warn Johnny-dog about the pool.

Little Johnny-dog wobbled across the patio, heading

for the door, but staggered off the edge and right into the water! He didn't make much of a splash, but fast as lightning, Yip jumped in and snatched him from the deep. Time for Poppi to get the towels again.

What a homecoming! There must be something to gettin' dunked when you get a new life. Johnny-dog sure looked surprised. He's never liked water since.

After a nice warm bath (being very careful of his stitches), a good meal in his tummy, antibiotics, and a hefty pain pill taking effect, Johnny-dog snuggled in a doggie blanket in Yip's arms until he fell asleep. He got his own crate right next to mine in the kitchen.

Yip kept us apart from the rough and tumble of puppy-play for what seemed like forever. I wanted to have fun, but he needed time to heal.

Yip and I still went for our long walks, but we only took Johnny-dog for short ones. Sometimes he'd just sit down with that pained look in his eyes, and Yip had to pick him up and carry him back home with me in tow. When Yip and I walked alone, she always wanted me to slow down, and to "stop practicing for the Iditarod."

Iditarod? With the snow, ice, and big dogs? Naw, this was, puppy-power walkin'! (I taught Johnny-dog how to do that when he got better.) The only big problem with walking the two of us at the same time is Yip and Johnny-dog always want to go the opposite of where I want to go. She had to buy us halters so we could tug and pull without choking. Much better.

We also got new sweaters from Santa for when it was cold. Winter does get cold in Florida. Johnny-dog got a red one with a big white bone on the top and mine was blue and white striped, with two bones on the top. We both look very sharp and collegiate.

We met many friends as we walked through the neighborhood: Susie, a Bichon Frise; Tennyson, an

Airedale; Scoobie Doo, a Yorkshire terrier; Samantha, a Maltese; and Mel, my bestest human friend who lived across the street and always had cookies in his pocket.

In comparison to all the doggies we've met, Yip calls me unique. I like that. Of course, I'm still not sure how she meant it, 'cause she also called me a 'pistol' and sometimes I heard the words 'a piece of work.' I really haven't figured those out.

Johnny-dog was getting better every day, but we had a problem with his name since Poppi was also named Johnny. Having two Johnnies in the house could be real confusing.

So, armed with a plan, Yip sat down one day with Johnny-dog. Going down the alphabet, speaking different names that appealed to her, she came to "Micky." Johnny-dog's ears perked up and his eyes went wide and joyful. I was quite sure he smiled. Problem solved. Johnny-dog became Micky.

I approved. Saying Max and Micky had a nice ring to it, too.

I taught Micky how to be house-trained. He originally came from a puppy mill, later transferred to a pet shop that was raided and closed, then to a rescue cage, so he never knew how to "do it" proper. I told him it's simple, really. First, you look anxious, then dance around a little bit, and next Yip comes running to the gate, saying, "Out? Potty? Out?" Kinda neat when you think about it.

Turns out, having Micky around was even better than being an only dog. Having a playmate is awesome. I shared all my toys with him. We had plenty of stuffed animals to chew on, a few chewy, hard rubber doggie things that Yip sometimes stuck a treat in, and a long orange lizard. Most of our toys squeaked, rolled, or bounced, but I loved my empty cottage cheese container the best, and Micky loved the lizard.

Micky gained weight and began to take longer walks and meet other people and their pets, but since he was a rescued dog, he hadn't been blended into dog society too well. Even to this day, we have to be careful in greeting new dogs. I get to say "hello" first, then he gets his nose touches and tail sniffs.

Before Micky came to live with us, Yip had hired a dog trainer. Poppi and I thought I was just fine, but Yip just wasn't on the same wavelength as we were.

The trainer said it was something in the voice. His methods were quite different from Yip's, and she vacillated between his ways and hers. She had five or six books about Australian terriers and on dog training, but at this writing, I think she gave most of them away.

Gee, I tried to let her know how to train me…just let me do everything my way.

Did I mention that I'm a very good watchdog, astute, and ready for action? Oh, and I don't fancy being combed or brushed for too long, and don't hold me under my chin or touch my feet. And no tummy rubs.

Of course, Micky loves all of that.

But back to the trainer, I know she paid good money for a professional, and she followed his ideas and actions the best she could under the existing circumstances. He did leave her with great hope and enthusiasm, though, for I already knew "Sit." However, I wasn't all that keen on "Stay," "Wait," or "Off." I preferred to pay attention to things of more importance like, "Cookie," "Yum-yums," "Walkies," and "Ridies."

In spite of the so-called training, life seemed pretty good. I was getting used to the "getting trained" and Micky was getting used to his new home, and Yip and Poppi were getting used to two puppies—but just before my first Christmas…

Three

Something was happening with Poppi, something unsettling. Dogs have a special instinct within them that makes them gifted in sensing things. I've heard cats have it too, but I can only speak for canines.

Several times during my first year, bright colored lights swirled outside the front window, and lots of quiet, hushed voices and strange smells came inside. Each time, Yip put us in our bedroom cages before the paramedics arrived so we wouldn't be in the way or get too upset; but I was upset. Poppi needed me! I barked and barked.

In February of 2007, they came again and took Poppi away to a place they called "hospital" for about three weeks. His kids and Yip's kids flew down to visit even before he was home.

When he returned, I made sure I slept near his legs while he was on the patio lounge, or between his knees when he was in his big, comfy recliner in the living room. I stayed by him more and more.

About mid-March, a very sweet lady visited Poppi. She came several times a week after that and Poppi always looked forward to her visits. She took out a long tube with a button on the end and placed on his chest, listening to his heart, lungs, and such. She wrote lots of notes and talked with him while I sat close by, or listened from my cage. She really liked me, too.

Life was changing. Yip had to help Poppi more and more, and she also had to lift me up to him on many occasions, especially onto his tall, new hospital bed in the front bedroom.

He still had his comfortable chair in the room, which was nice because it was low enough for me to jump up without hurting him.

I knew I had to guard Poppi and comfort him. I made sure to stick close with him more than usual, but all this moving of furniture, strange smells, and people in and out upset me. I huddled close to him, making it easy for him to hold me and let me lick him — even on his face, which wasn't really allowed. (We kept these licks a secret from Yip.)

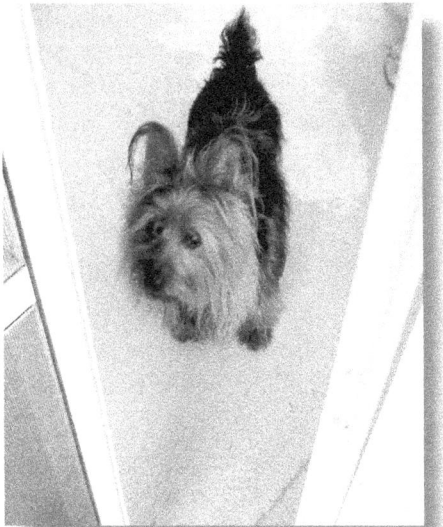

I took my job seriously. I'd only come out of his room if I had to go for walks, or potty, or to bed at night. Sometimes we even ate together. Of course, I had my real food in the kitchen with Micky, while Poppi had his in the bedroom, but we had yum-yums together. Poppi would have Jello or pudding, and I'd have a carrot. Micky would visit and check to see if everything was okay and if we'd left him any tidbits.

The worry was getting to me by May, and I needed several vet visits. June was even more stressful. I took good care of Poppy, but my anxiety was causing problems with my stomach, intestines, skin, ears, and teeth. More vet visits. More stress for me because, when I was at the vet's, I wasn't with Poppi. Sigh.

During the last week of June, Poppi got weaker and more tired and had to stay in his room all the time. Yip was sad and worried. Micky did his best to look after her for me. Many times, Yip, Micky, and I snuggled on the couch, Micky on her right, and I always sat on the left, closest to Poppi's room. We'd be real still as she whispered calming words to us. We'd look at her face quizzically, searching for some meaning to all we were experiencing.

The paramedics came again July first. The time had come for a decision. Poppi needed to go to the hospital or have round-the-clock nursing by Hospice. Yip said she knew he wanted to be home.

New people came to visit from Hospice and stayed with us all day and night.

Poppi's son, John Ty, arrived from his home in Bermuda late that night of July second. For several hours and all the next day, John Ty told Poppi all about Bermuda, friends, family, and other matters I couldn't understand.

I heard Yip and John Ty tell Poppi he was free to go whenever he wanted.

Go? Walkies? Yes! Come on, Poppi, get up!

But we didn't go walkies. I stayed ready, though.

Around four in the morning on July fourth, people were talking loudly, rushing around, asking questions, fixing tubes and tanks. Someone said there had been an oxygen blockage. John Ty switched tanks and warmed the lines. Once everything was adjusted, Poppi settled back into his chair, with Bill, the night-nurse, close by.

All was calm again, so Micky and I took a break to eat in the kitchen, and John Ty and Yip had just settled down with coffee in the living room.

Then, in less time than it takes a dog to sneeze, I went on alert.

Nurse Bill came into the living room and said, "He passed." Our people jumped up, talking all at once, and hurried to Poppi's room. Once again, tension filled the house like invisible, sharp, overwhelming static electricity. I sensed a dire, cataclysmic happening.

Passed? What? Wait! Where's everyone going? I didn't understand — Poppi wasn't to do anything without me! Things were really strange that morning, but what's this? I had to get out! I pawed at the gate and barked and barked, cried and scratched incessantly at the barrier.

That cataclysmic happening was separation.

"Hey! Somebody come! Yip, let me out!" I yelped and barked.

Bill's report said Poppi died at home, July 4, 2007, at 7:15 in the morning. No love or care by me or by anyone could stop his leaving.

I howled over and over from behind the gate, "Ouul, wouul, ouul!"

No one heard me or understood that I needed to be with him! I yowled and barked, overwhelmed by all the emotions and shock of my people. I whined and carried on, panting and pacing, jumping up and scratching at the fence, determined to get out.

At last, Yip realized I needed to be with Poppi. She picked me up over the gate and took me to him, leaving Micky in the kitchen. She gently set me beside Poppi, and I stretched out like usual. His hand touched me and smoothed my head and ears.

I didn't know it at the time, but Yip had lifted his arm and laid it around me, carefully patting and stroking my head with his hand. I felt some peace, but I kept looking towards his quiet face, wanting him to know that I was on the job, like usual, and all was okay now that I was there.

Nurse Bill made a call, and all too soon it was time for me to leave my Poppi, his bed, his room. He was my master for only one and a half years! I needed more time!

I fought to stay with him, but Micky and I were put in our crates in the big bedroom. The door was shut. We both barked and howled for Poppi. Other people came to our home.

Poppi was gone.

Bill said that Poppi had winked at him, closed his eyes, and left. In the twinkling of an eye, he was gone.

Yip said my Poppi went to greet all the other dogs he had told me about: Tippy, Duke, and Scruffy, and he'd meet Yip's dogs there, too: Wags, Scooter, Scruffy, Joshua, Holly, and Duffy.

John Ty had to fly back to Bermuda in a few days, but he helped Yip the rest of that week.

Poppi's things disappeared, the compressor, hoses, tanks, that big bed, even the carpet was taken up. More changes, new smells, more unknowns.

I clung to Yip just like Micky.

Four

Well, if things weren't already bad enough for Yip, I got sick, bad sick. I had to be rushed to the emergency animal hospital. The vet called my illness by some big name, but actually, I was sick at heart way down deep into my doggie soul. I mourned the loss of my Poppi for a very long time.

I had to have special everything: canned food, dry food, beige pills, gray pills, and a "quiet pill" which Yip threatened to take herself if I didn't get well soon enough. I was really sick in the hospital for about a week, and it took over three months before my whole insides were almost "normal," and then a year to fully recover. It also must have been expensive because Yip calls me her "million-dollar dog." Of course, it didn't cost a million dollars, but maybe close in doggie bucks.

Well, a great deal has happened since Poppi left us.

Yip cried often, but I knew what to do. I scooted right up to her when I could, joining with Micky to lick her tears. She'd hug us both and laugh some, almost like old times.

For many months, I'd search for Poppi in the house or when we were out on our walks, especially when a golf cart drove by. One time I broke away and followed an old man down the street, but he wasn't Poppi, and he wasn't very nice either.

After an unexpected mishap away from home, I needed surgery on my right hind leg, having total tendon replacement and some repair on another tendon with fishing line or something, I think. The vet said I had very unique knees, too. Yip grumbled something like, "Wouldn't surprise me." The vet just laughed. The other day at my checkup, he said I had "the pointiest knees he's ever known." Gosh! In a class by myself, right? Proves I'm as special as I always knew. I bet I'm her two million-dollar dog by now.

Recovery was rough. I had to stay in my crate for two weeks solid after surgery, only being lifted out and set down outside for potty while being kept on a very, very short leash. I was still in the crate for four more weeks with some limited exercise time in the gated kitchen. I had to take those "quiet pills" because I wasn't supposed to be too active. My body had to heal.

Yip enforced the vet's orders. She even used the flat furniture dolly from the garage to wheel me and my crate around from room to room so I wouldn't be lonely. A life of ease and luxury, right? But for an Australian terrier? No way. I needed to play with Micky and boss him around, chase ducks and rabbits, and most importantly, guard Yip and make sure she took long, fast walks.

Six weeks later, I was able to hobble out front and see Mel. He's the man! I got a cookie.

Sadly, long, fast walks were history. It took another few months to get me just to take little walks. Even now, my legs tire easily, so I just stretch out on the cool green grass wherever we might be…or once in a while, when my knees really hurt, or when tired, I stop walking and sit down and give my best pitiful look. Yip lightly pats me and says, "We'll take a break."

I know I'm not supposed to jump, but I still do sometimes because I'm a terrier. Plus, it keeps Yip on her toes and practicing the commands she likes best. "Off… down. Max, stop! Hey, no. Max? Are you listening? I'll get the fly swatter!"

As I said earlier, she sure is funny, and I just grin and pant and let her know she's doing a great job. By the way, don't worry, she really doesn't use a fly swatter.

Micky and I both adore her very much. We pant, perk our ears, and give her plenty of loving looks. She laughs and gives us a tiny doggie cookie or a baby carrot. She says I'm the only friend she's bought with money and can bribe with cookies and carrots. Micky never has a problem. He sits, follows orders, and Yip says he's the perfect doggie. It's not that I can't learn from him, you know, but when you're already Max the Great…

In the summer of 2009, we moved to a smaller

home. Micky and I didn't like seeing boxes and furniture leave our old home day after day and week after week as Yip moved our belongings, but the new home had a grassy, fenced yard with a nice view of a lake full of ducks, herons, cranes, and even the occasional feral pig to bark at. From time to time, Yip took us over to our new place so we could pee in the yard and smell our things in all the new rooms. We lost our pool, but the big floor tiles were nice and cold against my tummy. I think everything suited us three.

And we didn't lose all our friends. We discovered that Scooby Doo and his new baby brother, Spike, lived right across the street! We were all happy to see each other, but I know they were especially delighted to see me!

Micky and I made new friends: Big Max, Daisy, Brandy, and Bailey. During the "snowbird" season, about twenty-eight dogs lived on our street. Sniffing out all the neighborhood news could take a dog a whole day! Thankfully, of all us who live here full time get along pretty good, and Micky and I like running into all of them except one. Sigh, seems there's always "a rotten apple in every barrel." (Or a nutty dog on every street.)

In 2013, we moved again. I miss my fenced yard, but no fences means we can make sure Yip takes her walks. Well, I supervise, and Micky makes sure she walks. We have new friends here, a very old dog that Yip calls Princess, and sister and brother Yorkie mixes, Taz and Munchie. They are furry balls of puppy terrier energy. Yip says she feels for the owner. I think they're doing fine.

Some things haven't changed. We still miss Poppi. I look for him when we go out walking and have introduced myself to a few men who do kinda remind me of the good times. They're nice.

Yip still complains about me being "untrainable, in her face, an opportunist, a moocher, and, oh yeah, mischievously annoying." Gee, I thought being clever, cuddly, and quick were positive traits. I'm very careful to show her just how much I love her cooking, especially the bits she means to eat.

Of course, I do endeavor to keep her physically active, mentally alert, and emotionally fresh. Hmmm, guess I'll just have to pant, perk up my ears and look real innocent, so she can say what she always whispers to me, "Oh Max, you're just too cute!"

Yeahhh … I know.

Micky's cute, too, but I'm still the Alpha dog — tops at barking orders, always brave, alert, and forever loving — for I'm Max, the wonderful Australian terrier.

I could tell you more: there's that mishap with the bee, and of course, there was the golden rat snake adventure, but I think I'd better wait on those — gosh, almost forgot, I finally saw the raccoons. This big one rose up on his hind feet and hissed, and we all ran to the house for safety. As you know, I'm clever and brave, but I'm positive he was as big as a bear. Since I have to protect Yip, retreat was the wisest option.

Thank you for reading my story. I'd like to sign this last page with a paw print 'cause Yip likes them better than nose prints.

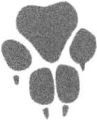

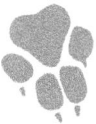

Five

Dear Readers, shortly after we moved in August, I noticed that Max was ravenous, losing weight, and drinking a tremendous amount of water … and what went in also went out.

Max was diagnosed with diabetes. We put him on insulin, and Max must have known it was good for him because after each meal he'd stand by me and wait for his shot. He had his blood work done often and his insulin needs were adjusted more frequently than was "normal."

Sadly, Max's always-upbeat attitude changed. He began to snap and bite Micky for no reason. Sometimes Max stared Micky down, and Micky would slink away or hide. A few times when I'd reach to give him a pat, he'd snap at my hand. I had figured he either was in pain and/or the illness was affecting his behavior mentally, too. I thought he could also be losing his peripheral sight. He was ill. He was not himself.

The vet and I were very honest with one another through that year, and he said we were getting near the "time" but making the decision regarding Max and his lifespan was up to me.

After all Max and I had been through together, this was

an extremely traumatic decision for me. We had a special bond, something intangible; no words could adequately explain Max. He loved everyone, and everyone loved him, no matter where we went. Emotionally, he was my "living" connection to Johnny.

The day for that decision came on December 12. Disease-wise, it had been a rough week for Max. He was failing. I called the vet that morning. It was his time.

I tried to make our last "ridy" happy. He was excited and ready to go. I lifted him up into the seat, buckled him in as usual and kissed him on the top of his head. The day was overcast, the thick cloud cover appearing to promise rain, despite the forecast. It was an odd day all around.

Max was his old bouncy self as he made the rounds of the bushes at the vet's, smelling messages left behind by other dogs and leaving his own.

Following is a letter that I'm sure Max would have written upon arrival in doggie heaven after his passing if stamps were valid from there.

December 25

Dear wonderful people at my vet's who touched me, shaved a leg or two, took my temperature, washed my backside (if needed), shortened toenails, brushed me, fed me food and water, dribbled medications and gave shots, cleaned my ears and my teeth (look up tartar in the dictionary and I bet you'll see a picture of my teeth), and blew me kisses. Thank you soooo much for making me feel better during all my visits to you in my short life span. (My ninth birthday would have been in the beginning of January.) I loved being with you all.

It's wonderful to finally be really free and sniff the great scents of the universe, so much better than mere

Earth's bushes and trees, or wherever other doggies have left messages.

Of course, nobody on Earth really knows about the scents of the universe, or of the souls of doggies, whether they just "die" with the furry stuff, or they are whisked off to a special place on angel's wings because of God's love. The Good Book says for human thinking, "No eye has seen, no ear has heard, no mind has conceived what God has prepared for those who love Him." (1 Corinthians 2:9, based on Isaiah 64:4 and 65:17)

Perhaps this letter might ease some broken hearts and give a little peace to those who mourn for beloved pets. Let me tell you of the happenings when my Yip left your office from my vantage point.

The old towel with my lingering smell was still on the front seat, and I was hoping she'd be okay to drive back to Micky. I don't know if you remember, but that morning, thickish clouds totally hid the sky. As my Yip was driving on Route 1, three holes, one on top of another, opened up towards heaven, and she could see blue through them. Being an emotional and spiritual person, she attributed the "holes" as one to God, the middle to the Son and the third to the Holy Spirit, thanking them for my life and the times we had together (although, I'm sure she'll never own another terrier). They say the mold was missing after I was made, but I think it was broken.

Slowly, the center hole elongated with wings rising from each side, becoming as an angel. Through her tears, she envisioned my doggie-soul riding on that angel's wings to Poppi. The angel shape and the other openings remained for a long time, even after she arrived home.

I knew Micky would be thrilled at her arrival, and cheer her up with his barking and jumping around. It was a good thing that they went for a walk, for another joyful surprise was happening in the sky for them, and maybe, for others as well. Yip kept looking up towards heaven at the angel. Near the end of their walk, with the top and bottom smaller holes still remaining round, the angel shape slowly opened both wings upwards and became a cross, with clouds filling in the winged areas for absolute definition. Well, by then she probably thought she was either cracking up or hallucinating … especially through blinding tears, but later that afternoon, she heard that at the time she saw the cross, other people had as well.

I figured Micky would take on the role of being the Alpha Dog right away. Although, being the nice dog that he is, Micky did look behind him before jumping up into Yip's lap for 'alone time' and hugs for several days afterward. (I didn't give him much space to do that while I was ill.) Well, I'm sure the two of them will get used to new routines and new experiences and much happiness.

Lots of zip kisses to all! Hope you like my photo. I was healthy then. Blessings to everyone for the coming New Year and for many, many more!

Max (the Great)

Thank you for reading.

If you wish to help support the future good health of Australian Terriers, please contact or send a contribution to the Australian Terrier Trust, c/o Kreg Hill, PO Box 5767, Palm Springs, CA 92263-5767. A portion of the proceeds from the sale of this little book about Max will be sent to the ATT in his memory.

Would you like to know when my next book is available? You can connect with me online online at:

inalouisejones.wordpress.com
twitter.com/inalouisejones

I would appreciate it if you would help others enjoy this book, too.

Lend it. Please share it with a friend.

Recommend it. Please help other readers find this book by recommending it to friends, readers' groups, and discussion boards.

Review it. Please tell other readers why you liked this book by reviewing it. I appreciate all reviews.

About the Author

I na Louise Jones has written and been involved with Bible studies and retreat programs for many years, growing up in the Christian faith from Sunday school Cradle Role to leader/ teacher. She also assisted with the writing of short letters of praise and hope for incarcerated young adults in California and in Florida.

After much interest from friends, Ina crafted a family devotional, *YRU,* to be published late 2017. She continues her passion to make theological truths more clearly understood in a fun and creative way for children and for adults.

She also writes short stories and articles. *Dah Dih Dah,* (w/a Ina Thurmond) a humorous article for CQ Magazine, early 70's; *Where There's Lightning,* (w/a Ina L. Jones) a personal true love story, SHE magazine, 2008; *One Man's Legacy*, a story of a prodigal, won 4th place in the 2011 Tom Howard contest; *Christmas, Once Again*, Evangel, Spring 2013; *One Dog, One Woman, One Day,* a short humorous story, The Saturday Evening Post, September 2014; and *The Wait,* a short story, The Florida Writer, April 2015.

She is a current member of the Vero Beach Chapter of Word Weavers International, the Palm City Chapter of the Florida Writers Association, the Morningside Writers Group, and the Cummings Library Writers' Group.

She loves interior decorating and photography. She has lived in California, Bermuda, and New Jersey, and now resides in Florida with her Poodle/Schnauzer who knows instinctively when to pester with unequaled doggedness for treats and walks.

www.ingramcontent.com/pod-product-compliance
Lightning Source LLC
Chambersburg PA
CBHW021118020426
42331CB00004B/550